The Respiratory System

CHRISTINE TAYLOR-BUTLER

Children's Press®
An Imprint of Scholastic Inc.
New York   Toronto   London   Auckland   Sydney
Mexico City   New Delhi   Hong Kong
Danbury, Connecticut

Content Consultant
Lawrence J. Cheskin, M.D., F.A.C.P.
Associate Professor of Medicine
Johns Hopkins University School of Medicine
Baltimore, Maryland

Library of Congress Cataloging-in-Publication Data

Taylor-Butler, Christine.
 The Respiratory system / by Christine Taylor-Butler.
      p. cm. -- (A true book)
  Includes index.
      ISBN-13: 978-0-531-16862-2 (lib. bdg.)
                  978-0-531-20736-9 (pbk.)
      ISBN-10: 0-531-16862-x (lib. bdg.)
                  0-531-20736-6 (pbk.)

 1. Respiratory organs--Juvenile literature. 2. Respiration--Juvenile literature.
I. Title. II. Series.

QP121.T39 2008
612.2--dc22   2007036021

Produced by Weldon Owen Education Inc.

1 2 3 4 5 6 7 8 9 10 R 17 16 15 14 13 12 11 10 09 08

Find the Truth!

Everything you are about to read is true *except* for one of the sentences on this page.

Which one is **TRUE**?

T or F The left lung is smaller than the right lung.

T or F Adults usually take a breath about 60 times a minute.

Find the answers in this book.

Contents

 When you sneeze, you always close your eyes!

4 Take a Deep Breath

Oxygen plus nutrients
equals energy.

CHAPTER 1

Catching Your Breath

You are swimming the final lap of a race. You surge toward the finish line. Your arms begin to ache. Your heart pounds in your chest. Your lungs tell you to stop. The race ends. You take huge gulps of air to "catch your breath," even though you've been breathing the whole time.

An adult takes 12 to 20 breaths a minute. During exercise, that might increase to 60 breaths a minute.

What's Going On?

Your body needs fuel for energy. Your blood gets oxygen from your lungs. It transports the oxygen around your body to your cells. The cells combine oxygen with nutrients from the food you eat. This produces energy.

Carbon dioxide is a waste product produced by this process. Your blood takes the carbon dioxide from your cells and sends it to your lungs. Then you breathe it out of your body.

Green plants use the sun's energy, carbon dioxide, and water to produce sugars and oxygen. They release the oxygen into the air.

When you exhale, your body gets rid of carbon dioxide.

9

When you exercise, the cells in your body burn oxygen faster in order to provide more energy. You breathe heavily to replace the oxygen you use, and to rid your body of the carbon dioxide more quickly.

Can you stop breathing? Not for long! Your cells would die without oxygen. Your brain would suffer damage without oxygen. Your body is smart. It knows what it needs. It knows how to get it. If you tried to stop breathing by holding your breath, your body would force you to take a breath.

Air Supply

Our lungs are designed to process air, not water. They cannot absorb enough oxygen from water. Deep-sea divers need an air supply. They use SCUBA gear. SCUBA stands for "self-contained underwater breathing apparatus." SCUBA cylinders usually contain a mixture that is the same as ordinary air. The mixture is about 78 percent nitrogen, 21 percent oxygen, and one percent other gases.

SCUBA diving can be dangerous. If you rise to the surface too fast, the nitrogen dissolved in your blood will form bubbles. This can kill you. It is important to rise slowly, in stages.

The left lung is smaller than the right lung. This is because it must share space with the heart.

Heart

Right lung

Left lung

CHAPTER 2

How It All Works

When you inhale, or breathe in, a layer of muscle below your lungs pulls down. The muscle is called the **diaphragm** (DYE-uh-fram). This allows air to fill the lungs. Your ribs expand to make room in your chest. When you exhale, or breathe out, the diaphragm moves up, pushing air out of the lungs. Your chest falls. Your lungs deflate.

The lungs never empty completely. Some air always remains. This prevents the lungs from collapsing.

Breathe In

Your nose is lined with tiny hairs, called **cilia** (SIHL-ee-uh). They help filter out particles from the air you breathe. The particles include bacteria, mold, and dust. Your nose and mouth also warm the air and add moisture to it.

Air travels from the nose or mouth down the back of the throat, or **pharynx** (FA-ringks), to the voicebox, or **larynx** (LA-ringks). Then it goes down the windpipe, or **trachea** (TRAY-kee-uh), to the lungs.

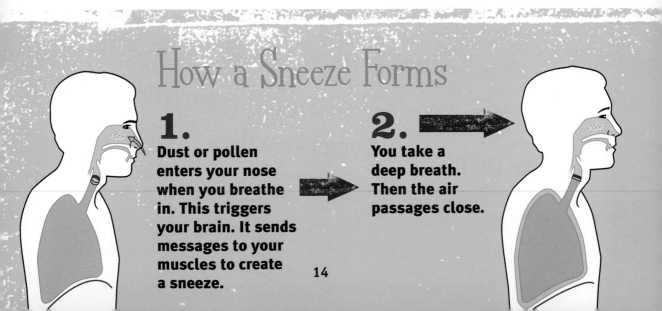

How a Sneeze Forms

1. Dust or pollen enters your nose when you breathe in. This triggers your brain. It sends messages to your muscles to create a sneeze.

2. You take a deep breath. Then the air passages close.

14

Breathe Out

When you exhale, your respiratory (breathing) system works in reverse. Your diaphragm relaxes and rises up. Your chest muscles also relax. This squashes the lungs. There is less space for air inside the lungs. The air is pushed out. It travels up the trachea and through the larynx and pharynx. Then it exits through your nose or mouth.

3.

Your diaphragm contracts, pressing against the lungs. The air is now under high pressure because the air passages are still closed.

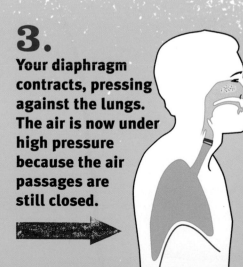

4.

You sneeze! The air passages open. Air rushes out of your lungs at about 100 miles an hour (160 kph). It usually carries anything in the air passages with it.

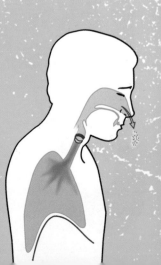

Say It Loud

The larynx has two small bands of tissue over it. They are called the vocal cords. When you speak, air passes over them. This causes them to vibrate. We learn to control them to make sounds that form speech or singing. The more forcefully you breathe out, the louder the sound.

Normally, you can speak or sing only when you breathe out, not when you breathe in.

If your lungs were removed from your body, they would shrink like deflated balloons.

Don't Choke

Your lungs are made to take in only air. There is a small flap of tissue at the back of your throat. It is called the **epiglottis** (ep-uh-GLOTT-uhss). This flap covers the larynx when you eat. It stops food and liquids from going down the windpipe. If they did, you would choke and could not breathe.

Bend It

The trachea, or windpipe, is a tube. It is lined with c-shaped rings of **cartilage** (KAR-tuh-lij). They keep the trachea from collapsing. Flexible tissue between the rings helps the trachea to bend as you move.

Cilia in the trachea are covered by **mucus** (MYOO-kuhss). The mucus traps any particles that get into the windpipe. The cilia move constantly. They push the mucus back up the trachea to the throat. The mucus is then swallowed.

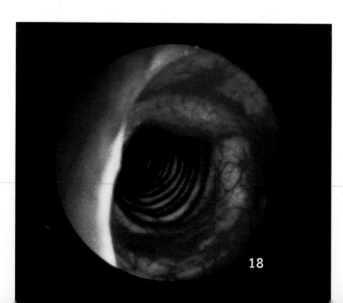

This is a magnified view down the trachea. It shows the rings of cartilage that hold it open.

Inside Your Lungs

Imagine your trachea as the trunk of a tree, upside down. At the bottom, the trachea splits into two main branches or tubes. These are called **bronchi** (BRONG-kee). One bronchus (BRONG-kuhss) enters the left lung. The other enters the right lung. Inside the lungs, the bronchi branch off into smaller tubes, called **bronchioles** (BRONG-kee-ohls). These tubes are as thin as hair. There are about 60,000 bronchioles in your lungs. They branch off into almost 700 million **alveoli** (al-vee-OHL-ee). Alveoli are air sacs.

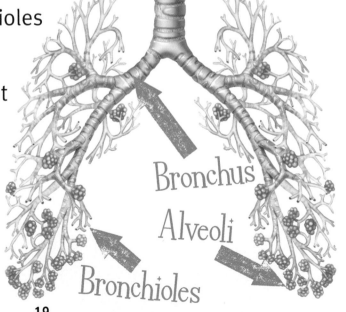

Trachea

Bronchus

Alveoli

Bronchioles

Tiny Balloons

Each alveolus is like a tiny balloon. It expands as it fills with air. The walls of the alveoli contain tiny blood vessels called **capillaries**. Both the walls and the capillaries are very thin. Oxygen and carbon dioxide can easily pass through them.

Inside the alveoli are white blood cells. These cells act like vacuum cleaners. They scoop up any germs or other particles that have managed to get into the lungs.

Alveoli

If you laid out all your alveoli so they were flat, they would cover a tennis court.

Carbon dioxide passes from the blood (blue blood vessels) into the alveoli. Oxygen passes from the air in the alveoli into the blood in the capillaries (red blood vessels).

Heart to Heart

Once the oxygen gets to your lungs, it needs to get around your body. Another organ helps with this process—the heart. The heart is a muscle that works like a pump for your body.

When oxygen passes through the walls of the alveoli, it is carried around the body in red blood cells. As these red blood cells travel around the body, they transfer oxygen to the body's cells. They also remove carbon dioxide. Then they carry the carbon dioxide back to the alveoli in the lungs. There they pick up a fresh supply of oxygen.

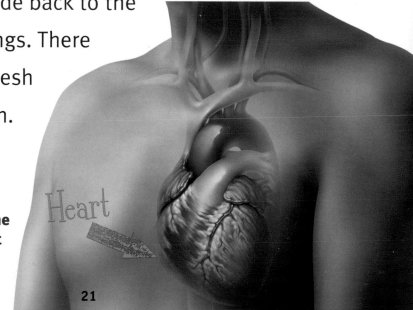

Without the heart to pump blood around the body, oxygen couldn't get to the cells.

Heart

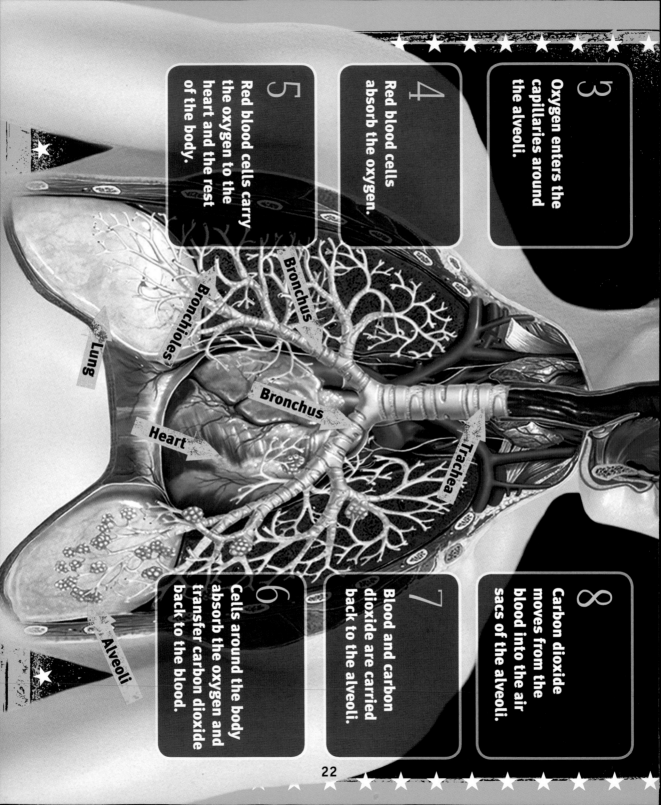

3
Oxygen enters the capillaries around the alveoli.

4
Red blood cells absorb the oxygen.

5
Red blood cells carry the oxygen to the heart and the rest of the body.

8
Carbon dioxide moves from the blood into the air sacs of the alveoli.

7
Blood and carbon dioxide are carried back to the alveoli.

6
Cells around the body absorb the oxygen and transfer carbon dioxide back to the blood.

Bronchus

Bronchioles

Bronchus

Lung

Heart

Trachea

Alveoli

Energy to Burn

You run. You jump. You laugh. You sneeze. You cough. You think. Without oxygen, you wouldn't be able to do any of those things.

1
Air containing oxygen is inhaled. It travels down the trachea.

2
Oxygen enters the bronchi, bronchioles, and alveoli.

10
Another breath of fresh, oxygenated air is inhaled.

9
The used air travels up bronchial tubes and then the trachea. It is exhaled through the nose or mouth.

When we yawn, we take extra oxygen into our bodies. This helps us become more alert if we are tired or bored.

CHAPTER 3

Evading the Defense

You breathe all the time. You don't even have to think about it. Your respiratory system works automatically. Cilia in your nose and trachea help keep out many germs, such as bacteria. Sometimes, however, things that make you sick get through the defense system. And sometimes lungs develop problems.

When you are asleep, you breathe more slowly than when you are awake. That is because your body doesn't need as much oxygen when you are asleep.

Achoo!

Most people get a cold or the flu at some time. These illnesses are caused by viruses. Colds can usually be treated by drinking plenty of fluids and resting. Most colds aren't transferred by touching. They are caused by breathing in a cold virus. The virus enters the air when someone sneezes or coughs. Coughing and sneezing are your body's way of clearing out the germs and mucus that build up in your nose, throat, and lungs.

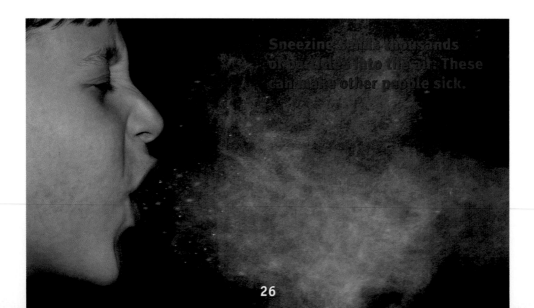

Sneezing sends thousands of particles into the air. These can make other people sick.

Wash Your Hands

One of the best ways to prevent colds and flu from spreading is to turn away from people and cover your mouth when you cough or sneeze. This helps keep the germs from spreading through the air. Use a handkerchief or tissue when you blow or wipe your nose. But that's not all you should do to keep yourself and others safe. Always wash your hands with warm, soapy water to remove germs. Then dry your hands well. More germs are transferred from wet hands than clean, dry ones.

This is one of the viruses that cause colds.

There are more than 200 types of cold viruses.

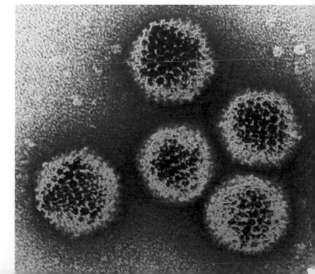

Allergies

An allergy is a reaction by the body to a particular substance, called an allergen. The white blood cells that protect the body get a message that the substance is harmful. They then attack it.

Most respiratory allergies are caused by dust, animal dandruff, pollen, and mold. Someone who is allergic to these allergens can get a variety of symptoms when inhaling them. Symptoms include a runny nose, coughing, and sneezing.

Hay fever and other respiratory allergies can cause the eyes to water and itch.

28

Air Flow

Asthma (AZ-muh) is a kind of allergy. It affects a person's ability to breathe. When an asthma attack occurs, the muscles of the bronchial tubes contract. The lining of the air passages swells. These problems restrict the flow of air in and out of the lungs. This causes wheezing, coughing, and difficulty in breathing.

Treatment for asthma may include the use of inhalers. These quickly open up the breathing passages. This allows more air to be inhaled and exhaled.

CHAPTER 4

Take a Deep Breath

When you go for a checkup, the doctor may listen to your lungs using a stethoscope. He or she may ask you to take a deep breath and hold it. Then you will be asked to let the breath out slowly. This allows your doctor to check that there is no problem with your lungs. There are also tests that show how strong your lungs are.

If you live to be 70 years old, you will have taken about 600,000 million breaths!

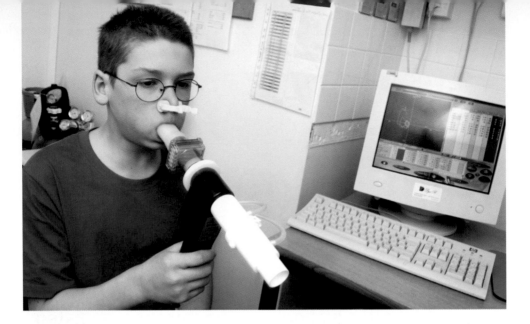

A spirometer measures how much air is going into, and out of, the lungs.

In some cases, a doctor will ask you to breathe into a special machine called a spirometer. This tests how much air your lungs can breathe in and out.

Exercise can increase the capacity of the lungs. Smoking and lung disease can reduce it.

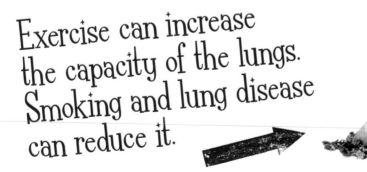

Respiratory Diseases

Pneumonia (noo-MOH-nyuh) is caused by an infection of the lungs. The alveoli fill with fluid. This prevents oxygen from being carried to the blood. If untreated, pneumonia can lead to death.

Emphysema (em-fuh-SEE-muh) is often caused by smoking. The walls of the alveoli become less stretchy. The alveoli cannot deflate. Therefore, they cannot rid themselves of carbon dioxide.

Bronchitis (brong-KYE-tiss) is usually caused by a virus. It makes the bronchial tubes swell. Bronchitis causes coughing, wheezing, and a sore chest.

If you have bronchitis, you keep coughing to clear the mucus out of your lungs.

Common but Deadly

Tuberculosis (tu-bur-kyuh-LOH-siss), or TB, is a serious disease caused by bacteria. In the past, it was one of the most common causes of death.

TB causes hard lumps to form in the lungs. It also causes coughing. TB is spread when someone breathes in bacteria coughed or sneezed into the air by a person with an active form of the disease.

Tuberculosis has been around since ancient times. Evidence of it has been found in Egyptian mummies!

About a third of the people in the world have TB bacteria in their bodies. The disease is highly contagious. However, most people who have it do not get sick from it.

If caught early, TB can be cured with antibiotic drugs. However, some people have a form of the disease that is resistant to drugs. They must follow special precautions, such as wearing masks This is to keep them from infecting other people.

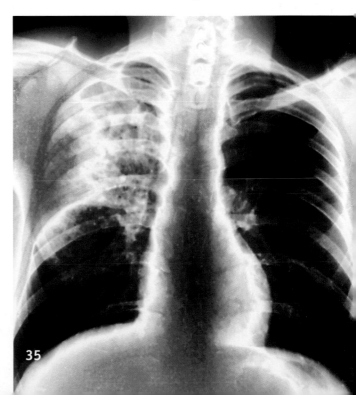

In this x-ray, the lungs (dark blue) have been damaged by TB (grainy, white patches).

Artificial Lungs and Transplants

Sometimes patients cannot breathe on their own. For example, they may need time for a lung infection to heal. These patients are placed on a ventilator. This is a machine that uses a mechanical pump to help the patient breathe in and out.

A ventilator helps this boy breathe as he recovers from heart surgery.

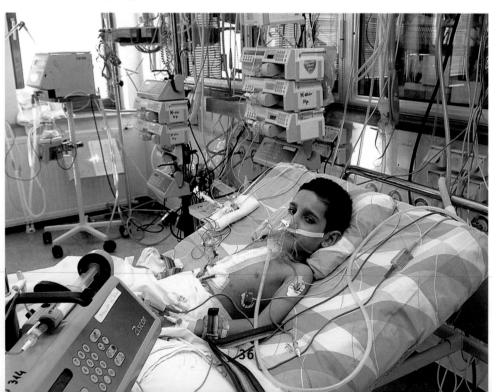

Sometimes people develop serious lung diseases that can't be treated. They may die if they don't receive a lung transplant. This is a healthy lung from someone who has died. The wait can be a long one. Sometimes it takes several years to find a donor with the same tissue type.

Scientists have invented an artificial lung. It can breathe for a patient until a lung is available for transplant. The lung is about the size of a soda can. It uses the patient's heart as a pump.

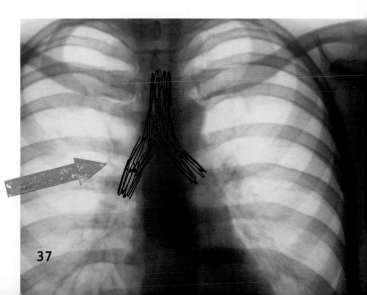

The cartilage of this patient's trachea became weak because of illness. A tube called a stent has been inserted to keep the airways open.

Stent

Saving a Life

Cardiopulmonary resuscitation (CPR) is used to keep alive a person who has stopped breathing. It helps keep oxygen flowing through the body until medical help arrives. CPR must be performed within four minutes. Otherwise, the person may suffer brain damage from lack of oxygen. CPR can save lives. However, it can be dangerous if performed on a person who is still breathing.

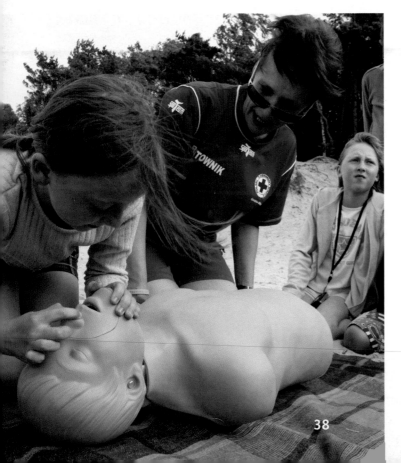

Many people take a class to learn how to perform CPR. This girl is practicing on a dummy.

Smoking

When people smoke, toxic chemicals are absorbed into their lungs. These chemicals then pass into the bloodstream. They circulate through the body. They can reach the brain in about eight seconds. The chemicals in tobacco smoke destroy lung tissue. They can cause cancer and other respiratory diseases.

Even if you don't smoke, your lungs can be hurt by the smoke from people who do. Secondhand smoke is smoke breathed out by people smoking nearby. Babies and children who are exposed to secondhand smoke can develop asthma and other diseases.

Protect Your Lungs

Your lungs are the second largest organ in your body. They make direct contact with the environment—by exchanging air. Whatever is in the air can get into your body. So it's important not to breathe polluted air. It is also important to practice good habits so that you don't make other people sick.

In some places, air pollution is very bad. Sometimes people need to wear masks when they are outside.

Keep on Track

Try to breathe only clean air. Smoke from burning buildings, campfires, and barbecue pits contains harmful particles. Remember to keep your distance.

It is also important to reduce indoor air pollution. Dust and mold can trigger allergies. Sometimes the dust stays in your lungs and coats the bronchioles and alveoli. Then the alveoli are less able to transfer oxygen into your blood.

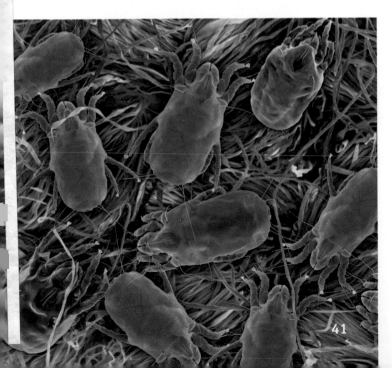

Dust mites live in dust. They cause allergies in some people. They can be seen with a microscope.

A mattress can have millions of dust mites living inside it.

When working on projects that will create dust or fumes, it is a good idea to wear a mask. This will protect your lungs. Never inhale air from balloons, glue, or aerosol cans. It can permanently damage your lungs. It can even kill you.

The best way to take care of your respiratory system is to get plenty of fresh air and exercise. ★

Number of breaths taken by a newborn baby:
Between 30 and 60 a minute

Number of breaths taken by an adult at rest:
Between 12 and 20 a minute

Number of children in the United States with asthma: About 6 million

Annual deaths in the United States from cigarette smoking: About 400,000

Annual deaths in the United States from secondhand smoke: About 40,000

Amount of mucus produced by the nose and sinuses each day: About 1 pint (0.47 liter)

Did you find the truth?

F Adults usually take a breath about 60 times a minute.

T The left lung is smaller than the right lung.

Resources

Books

Gold, Susan Dudley. *The Respiratory System*.
Berkeley Heights, NJ: Enslow Publishers, 2003.

Houghton, Gillian. *Breath: The Respiratory
System*. New York: PowerKids Press, 2007.

Keeffe, Emmet B., M.D. *Know Your Body:
The Atlas of Anatomy*. Berkeley, CA:
Ulysses Press, 1999.

Petrie, Kristin. *The Respiratory System* (Human
Body). Edina, MN: Checkerboard Books, 2006.

Silverstein, Dr. Alvin and Virginia, and Laura
Silverstein Nunn. *Smoking* (My Health).
New York: Franklin Watts, 2003.

Taylor-Butler, Christine. *The Circulatory System*.
(A True Book™: Health and the Human Body).
New York: Children's Press, 2008.

Winston, Robert. *The Human Body Book*.
New York: DK Publishing, 2007.

Organizations and Web Sites

Biology For Kids

www.biology4kids.com

Learn a little or as much as you like about biology.

ThinkQuest

http://library.thinkquest.org/5777/resp1.htm

Read a simple guide to the respiratory system.

Saskatchewan Lung Association

www.lung.ca/children/index_kids.html

Play games to learn about the respiratory system.

Places to Visit

Adventure Science Center

800 Fort Negley Blvd.
Nashville, TN 37203
615-862-5160
www.adventuresci.com/
exhibits
Visit the BodyQuest exhibit and see what goes on inside your body.

Science Museum of Minnesota

120 W. Kellogg Blvd
St. Paul, MN 55102
651-221-9444
www.smm.org/visit/
humanbody
Visit the Human Body Gallery and take a virtual tour of the lungs.

Important Words

alveolus (al-vee-OHL-uss) – an air sac that transfers oxygen to the blood vessels (plural: alveoli)

bronchiole (BRONG-kee-ohl) – a thin tube that leads to the alveoli

bronchus (BRONG-kuhss) – one of the two tubes that split off from the trachea (plural: bronchi)

capillary (CAP-uh-lehr-ee) – a very thin blood vessel

cartilage (KAR-tuh-lij) – firm, elastic tissue present in the ears and respiratory system. It is also present in joints.

cilia (SIHL-ee-uh) – tiny hair-like structures that line the airways and keep out particles

diaphragm (DYE-uh-fram) – the layer of muscle that helps inflate and deflate the lungs

epiglottis (ep-ih-GLOT-uss) – the small flap of tissue that can cover the windpipe to prevent you from choking on food

larynx (LA-ringks) – the air passage that contains the vocal cords

mucus (MYOO-kuhss) – a slimy substance that protects the respiratory system

pharynx (FA-ringks) – the tube that leads to both the larynx and the esophagus (the tube leading to the stomach)

trachea (TRAY-kee-uh) – the tube that carries air to the lungs

Index

About the Author

Christine Taylor-Butler lives in Kansas City, Missouri, with her husband and two daughters. A native of Ohio, she is the author of more than 40 books for children. She holds a B.S. degree in both Civil Engineering and Art and Design from the Massachusetts Institute of Technology in Cambridge, MA. Other books by Ms. Taylor-Butler in the True Book Health and the Human Body series include: *The Food Pyramid*, *Food Allergies*, *Food Safety*, *The Circulatory System*, *The Digestive System*, and *The Nervous System*.

PHOTOGRAPHS: Big Stock Photo (girl sneezing, p. 5; p. 8; p. 39); Getty Images (p. 26); iStockPhoto.com (© David Safanda, p. 11; ©Joshua Sherurcij, p. 34; © Nuno Silva, p. 43; © Paula Photographic, p. 16; © Stuart Brill, p. 29; © www.pmsicom.net, p. 3); Photolibrary (p. 18; p. 37; p. 42); Rubberball Production (boy, p. 5); Stock.XCHNG (back cover; p. 4; cigarette, p. 32; © Stacy Brasswell, p. 10); Tranz/Corbis (cover, p. 6; p. 9; p. 12; p. 17; p. 24; p. 30; p. 33; p. 36; p. 38; p. 41). All other images property of Weldon Owen Education.